I am **smarter** than you think, Mom and Dad

I am smarter than you think, Mom and Dad

How to raise responsible kids

Mridula Agarwal

BLUEJAY

Bluejay Books Pvt. Ltd.
A-8/76, Ist Floor
Sector 16, Rohini
Delhi 110 085
info@bluejaybooksindia.com

First published in 2014 by
Bluejay Books Pvt. Ltd.

Typeset by Eshu Graphic

Printed and bound in India

To my sons
Manal and Adhish...
They are my joy and my pride.

CONTENTS

AUTHOR'S NOTE

Having children makes you no more a parent than having a piano makes you a pianist.

— *Michael Levine*

Giving birth to a child may not be difficult, but to bring her up to become a responsible and mature individual capable of living a satisfying and happy life is by no means an easy task. And today's fast developing and changing world is making it even tougher. With easy access to information, that is not always good for the kids – which may also not be what their developing and impressionable minds can handle – and the inappropriate temptations they are exposed to today have made the job of parents even trickier. This has also put extra burden on them and they need to take their responsibility seriously. Besides, parents today are also likely to be busier with their own demanding schedules and may not always have enough time to guide their kids the way they should or would want to.

Very often parents feel that just as bringing a child into this world is a natural process, so would bringing her up be. They would automatically know what is good for their child and know how to take care of all her needs. They may also believe that their children will be so special that they will encounter no difficulty at all. They do not think of the unpleasant surprises a lot of parents come across and the problems arising out of them if they are not handled properly. And above all, they may also not be aware of their own role in shaping the lives of their children and may not set the right example.

The world out there is the same for every child but different children get influenced in different ways. Some develop a high level of maturity and compassion that is rare to come by while others grow up to become self-seeking and insensitive individuals. Some do well and live successful and happy lives, some drift through life with nothing to account for, while some take to drugs and crime and need help to stay out of trouble.

The first and foremost reality parents have to understand is that they are the chief guiding force in the lives of their children, and children learn more from observing and experiencing than from teaching and preaching. To start with, children are totally dependent on their parents or caregivers for all their needs – physical, emotional and spiritual – which makes the role of the adults in their life extremely important.

In today's demanding and challenging time, parents may not always find their own life skills adequate in handling their own affairs, and as such, may not be sure of the values they would want to instill in their children and how to go about it. No doubt times have changed, and so have our requirements, but the basic norms of right and wrong are still the same, and will always be.

Children learn from every experience; even the ones that may appear trivial to us are not always so for the child. Children have no preconceived notions and hold no prejudices and this helps them to see things as they really are. Children do not give their personal meaning to any incident as they do not have past experiences that could influence their interpretation, and, as such, their observation is sharper than we think it is. They are also likely to accept every happening just the way they encounter it and in the process learn it as the way of life.

> *Hypocrisy may deceive the cleverest man, but the least wide awake of children recognize it.*
>
> — *Leo Tolstoy*

This book deals with the most important task of raising responsible kids in this fast-paced and challenging world. All the major issues facing parents today have been carefully addressed. It will help you to understand the importance of the early years in the life of your kids and recognize their significance. It will also show you how everyday life events influence your children and how they can affect their personality for all times to come. These are real life events and can be more useful in helping you to understand how these seemingly insignificant occurrences could affect a tender mind. Care has been taken to explain what meaning a particular experience could have for your child and how your unintentional oversights could influence and shape his or her future.

Having a better insight into the mind of your child will help you realize the power you have over her, of which you may yourself not be aware of. By recognizing the implications of your actions and statements and the meaning they could have for your kid, you will be in a better position to take care of what you do and say, and what examples you set. When you take care to provide a healthy environment and set the right examples, it will help your children to grow into successful and responsible adults and lead satisfying and happy lives.

And when this happens, it will need no extra time or effort from you to raise responsible kids you can be proud of. You can then be a satisfied parent, happy at having done your most important job well which is the best reward any parent can aspire for.

If you bungle raising your children, I don't think whatever else you do well matters very much.

— Jacqueline Kennedy Onassis

THE FUSSY AND THE NAUGHTY CHILD

Almighty was sitting in his high chair, reflecting upon his work. His assistant Farishta sat beside him, listening carefully.

"I have created this world for people to be happy in. I have given them lovely kids who can be a source of great joy and happiness to them. People can bring up their children to become caring and responsible human beings but it is not really happening so. Parents are finding it difficult to instill proper values in their kids even when the little ones are so receptive, truthful, and accepting." Almighty sounded distressed.

"What can be the reason for this?" Farishta asked with concern.

"The reasons are many, but the main problem is that people do not treat their kids as individuals who can think and understand for themselves and will learn from what they see. Children's perceptions are keen, you know," explained Almighty. "You cannot fool them into believing what is not true. And what they are exposed to now, as little kids, is what they will learn and retain in their life for future."

"Is this the main cause of all the unhappiness we see in the world today?" Farishta wanted to know.

"Yes. When children are not brought up well, they grow up to become selfish and demanding adults. And selfish and demanding individuals can never be a source of great happiness to anyone, including themselves," reflected Almighty.

"I can understand that," said Farishta, "but what is it that the parents are doing wrong that is making their kids selfish and demanding? And what should they do differently to set it right?"

"First of all, parents should appreciate the value of the early years of the lives of their kids and take proper care of them at that time," said Almighty.

"But parents do take care of their kids when they are young; in fact, they pamper them and spoil them and, at times, even put up with so much nonsense from them that it amazes me," said Farishta, trying to understand this puzzling situation. "Besides, children can always learn and improve their ways after they grow up," he continued trying to be optimistic.

"No, changing your ways after you grow up is not easy. By the time a child is five years old, her basic personality is formed and then stays almost the same for the rest of her life," explained Almighty with concern.

"Oh! Really? This is something new to me and totally out of my comprehension. Can you explain it a little please?

I think a lot of parents will be glad to know something about it," Farishta enthused.

"Yes, I will elucidate it if you want. Though I feel most parents do know a little about how important the early years are. A lot has been written and said about it and I expect parents to be aware," said Almighty.

"Do you mean to say that the entire pattern of an individual's personality, for all times to come, is formed in the early years?" Farishta asked with surprise.

"Yes, that is exactly what I am trying to tell you. By the time a child is five years old, her pattern of life is almost set," said Almighty.

"But how much does a child understand by the time she is five years old?" asked Farishta trying his best to comprehend this complex situation.

"Go down to earth and find it out for yourself," suggested Almighty.

And Farishta flew down.

Farishta's descent was smooth. The day was still young and a pleasant morning breeze welcomed him. It was a beautiful day. A light shower had bathed the earth and it was fresh and cheery.

Farishta walked a few yards before he came across a lovely home with a beautiful garden. He saw a cute little girl sitting with her mother. The little one was sitting pretty with her mouth shut while her mother tried her best to make her eat something. The mother would fuss over the kid, entice her, scold her, or even threaten her, but the little girl just refused to open her mouth. Getting her to eat anything was simply impossible. Farishta felt sorry for the mother. How devoted and caring mothers can be and children give them so much trouble! His heart went out for all the devoted mothers of the world. It was simply unbelievable to see what pains mothers take for their children.

Farishta sat down next to the little girl and asked, "Why are you not eating anything dear, are you not hungry?"

"I am hungry," came a soft sweet reply.

"Then why don't you eat?"

"________________"

"Do you not like what Mummy is giving you?"

"________________"

"Are you angry about something?"

"________________"

"If you do not tell me what your problem is, then how will I know?" Farishta tried to be of help.

"There is no problem," whispered the little one as gently as she could.

"No problem? Then why are you not listening to your mother? Why are you not eating anything? Especially when you are hungry and also like what mummy is giving you." Farishta was astonished.

"Because I am not stupid."

"What? What did you say? You are not what?" Farishta wanted to make sure he had heard right.

"B-e-c-a-u-s-e, I am not stupid," repeated the little one softly, and then looking up at Farishta's confused face added, "Don't you know, if I eat, Mummy will leave me and go? How will I hold on to her if I do not fuss over my food?" asked the little girl innocently and Farishta was stumped. The little girl was indeed right; if she did not fuss over her food, how would she have her mother all to herself? Can little children really be so smart? He wondered.

"But you are hungry and also like what Mummy is giving you, then why don't you eat?" he probed further.

"Oh, I am used to being a little hungry at times, but I never starve. Mummy will go on offering me food and I will keep on eating a little at a time. Both Mummy and I are used to this pace, you know, and both of us like this arrangement too," whispered the little one truthfully.

Farishta was bemused. "What do you mean by both of you liking this arrangement? How can Mummy want to have you fussing over your food in any case?" he asked with surprise. But you cannot expect little kids to understand things as they really are. Can you? How much do they actually know? After all, they are so inexperienced and so small.

Then the little girl spoke again, with all the innocence and frankness of a little child that she was, and explained, "Oh, that is so easy to understand. When I want Mummy's attention, I hold on to her this way, and when Mummy wants to sit with me ignoring everything else, she fusses over me. She sits with me for hours and both of us are happy."

Farishta was dumbfounded. "This is simply unbelievable; can little children really be so smart?" he mused to himself and got up.

He set out to see some more kids around.

Farishta came across a market place; the market was busy and there was activity all over. He saw a cute little boy, about three years old, the apple of his mother's eye, sitting pretty in his push-chair, going round the market while his mother tried to shop. He was giving his mother a tough time. He would run around if she put him down, or stick his legs out and pull at things, and insist on getting out if she put him in.

Farishta went up to the little boy and asked him what he was up to. The little one looked up, smiled his cutest smile, and replied, "My Mummy is shopping and I am messing."

"What?? You are doing what?" Farishta found it difficult to believe his ears.

"I am messing," repeated the little one looking as innocent as he was.

"And what does messing mean?" Farishta was curious to know if the little one understood what he had said. After all, a child of three is not expected to understand the meaning of messing.

"I am being naughty," explained the little one truthfully, "I am troubling my mother and not letting her shop."

Farishta was astounded. The purity and honesty of the cute little one was amazing; his frankness remarkable. Kids are indeed innocent. But why should a kid want to trouble his mother? Farishta wondered and probed further. "And why are you being naughty?" he asked.

"Because I want my Mummy's attention," explained the little one with the simplicity and straightforwardness of a three-year-old.

"But don't you get your Mummy's attention at home?" queried Farishta.

"Yes, sometimes I do, but not always. That is why I try to keep her busy with me whenever she is around. She goes out for work and I do not like it at all," the little one was honest.

"But why are you demanding her attention in the market? She needs to shop here," Farishta persisted.

"Because this is the easiest way to get her attention. Besides, Mummy expects me to be naughty too," smiled the insightful, innocent three-year-old.

"Now, now, how can that be possible? Your Mummy can never want you to trouble her, I am sure of that," said Farishta.

"She does expect me to trouble her," insisted the little one with the purity and thoughtfulness of a smart little kid.

"Really? And what makes you believe so?" arishta quizzed with amusement, not expecting the little one to come up with any proper explanation.

"Oh! I know it because I have heard her say so many times. Just yesterday she was telling a friend of hers that I am very naughty and difficult, that I do not let her do anything and am always demanding her attention. I have to do what my Mummy expects me to do. If she thinks I am naughty, then I have to be naughty. Mummys are always right, you know," declared the little one with pride.

"But your Mummy was only complaining to her friends. She did not want you to be naughty. After all, no mother can want her kid to trouble her." Farishta tried to see sense and make his point.

"You do not seem to understand mothers at all," smiled the little child, "they never complain about their kids, they only take pride in them. A naughty kid is a smart kid and every Mummy tries to tell the other Mummy how her kid is naughtier than the rest. They talk about us at their kitty parties and dinner parties, during lunch break and tea break, at public functions and wedding receptions. All my friends know this too, and we want to make our mothers proud," explained the little one, standing straight as a proud soldier.

And Farishta was stumped again. How innocent and perceptive this little kid was! Like a devoted child he was doing what he thought his mother expected him to do. It was indeed commendable; Farishta was impressed. But was the little one right?

He could see the purity and honesty of the children he met, but the adults? The children were sure to be wrong about them. He found it difficult to understand what he saw. He went to a park and lay down on a bench to think, but slipped into a slumber instead. It was evening by the time he got up, and realizing the time, decided to have a quick round before he left.

A mother had just returned home from work. She called the nanny, "Has *Baba* eaten anything today? Has he had his milk and his vitamins?" she asked. And then, before the nanny could reply, added, "I know he must not have eaten anything, he is so fussy about his food. He must be starving, bring him to me," she said.

The little boy came in, hiding behind the nanny. The mother felt left out, and a little disappointed and guilty too. This was her kid showing more faith in his caregiver than his mother. But what could she do? After all, it was the nanny who looked after him the whole day. She knew she needed to take a break from work in the interest of her child. But how could that be possible? What would she do with her time and her talent if she quit her job? Besides, the household was now used to the extra income she was bringing in. She pulled the child to herself, hugged him, and asked, "What did you do the whole day today, my dear?" and getting no response from the kid added, "Have you eaten anything? Are you hungry? Should I order something nice for you? Whatever you say. Will you have a pizza or a burger? Or Chinese or Thai, or whatever you want?"

"I want ice-cream," said the little one.

"What? Just ice-cream? But there is a lot of ice cream in the fridge. Why did you not have it?" the mother was amazed.

"There was only butterscotch and vanilla and I hate them both. I want chocolate ice cream," he said.

The mother picked up the phone and ordered pizza and choco-chips. Then handing the kid over to the nanny, she went in to freshen up and change. By the time she came out, the pizza and the ice cream had arrived. But the boy would not eat. He did not want to have the ice cream either, was too full and not interested. He continued to watch *Spiderman* instead; he wanted to be like him. He had had sandwiches and milk, the nanny said, but the mother was not satisfied. She felt ignored and left out again. The boy did not appear to have missed her and was not even interested in eating what she had ordered for him. She tried her best to entice the child to eat something, but he ignored her and remained glued to the TV. The father walked in and the mother tried to enlist his help.

"He has not eaten anything today. I ordered pizza and his favorite ice cream but he is busy watching *Spiderman,*" she complained.

"This is all your fault. You have spoilt him so," said the father going in to change and relax. He needed his drink after such an exhausting day.

It was now getting late and Farishta decided to call it a day. There was a lot of fuss over kids' food he had seen, but he could not understand why. Children are growing up fast, and for proper development of their bodies and mind, they do need healthy and wholesome food. But why were they not eating? Farishta felt concerned. But somehow, to his amazement, they looked healthy. Thinking of this made him feel better. And what about the naughty child? Was his reasoning right? Farishta felt confused and needed answers. He decided to go up and ask Almighty. And he flew back.

Almighty was taking his evening walk when Farishta arrived. He saw the puzzled look on Farishta's face and smiled, "so, you have been busy today, I guess."

"Yes, indeed. I am totally bowled over by what I saw," admitted Farishta. "Those little ones are smart and innocent, they are simply loveable and cute, and they have their own reason and understanding. But they understand their parents wrong, I am sure," said Farishta with doubt. He was again thinking of the little boy he had spoken to.

"Children are seldom wrong," explained Almighty. "They have no preconceived notions and no prejudices, and their senses are keen. That makes them observant, receptive, and accepting. They know the world around them better than people think they do," he said.

"Do you mean to say that the little boy's mother is really proud of her son being naughty?" Farishta asked with surprise.

"Yes, that is absolutely right. A lot of mothers do feel proud to talk about their children's naughtiness and the kids know it. No mother ever criticizes her child, ever. In the guise of criticism, they are always trying to make a statement. They very wrongly feel that it is smart and normal for a child to be naughty and difficult. They forget that the children will grow up to be what they make them to be as kids, they cannot be otherwise. Children seldom do anything wrong on their own," said Almighty.

"Then what made the *messing* three-year-old misbehave?" asked Farishta.

"Three years old never misbehave. A misbehaving three-years-old is an adult misconception. Whatever they do is learnt behaviour. They simply do things that interest them, or what they think adults expect from them, or what brings the desired response from the adults, or what they see them doing," explained Almighty.

"But the child knew he was messing, and he did it on purpose to get his mother's attention," Farishta persisted.

"Yes, children do misbehave at times, and, mind you, this is learnt behaviour, to get the result they are looking for. But they do it only when they do not get what they want otherwise. Or when they feel that is what the adults expect from them," clarified Almighty, and continued, "Do not forget that this child was being naughty both to get his mother's attention and to come up to her expectations as well. He knew his mother was, in a way, proud of his naughtiness," explained Almighty

"I can't understand how any mother can feel proud of her child being naughty. Do they really do?" asked Farishta with disbelief.

"Yes, a lot of them do feel proud of their children being naughty. They confuse a naughty child with a creative child who is brought up with love and care and who goes out to explore the world without hesitation. As her curious and experimental ways are likely to get her into trouble time and again, she gets labelled as naughty. And when this child turns out to be smarter than the other kids, the mothers think that naughty kids are smarter kids," explained Almighty.

"So that is the reason why parents feel that the naughtier a child is, the smarter she is. But what is the rationale behind this misconception? Can you explain it a little further for me please?" asked Farishta.

"Yes, I can," said Almighty. "There is a subtle difference between a curious child and a naughty child and that needs to be understood properly. The mother of a curious child has the interest of her child in her mind and she encourages her to explore her surroundings with the idea to allow her to experiment and learn on her own while she is there for her whenever needed. This promotes creativity which can go a long way in later life. On the other hand, the mother who takes pride in her child being naughty does so to make a statement. And, in the bargain, she inadvertently teaches her child to be naughty where all that he wants is to seek attention. And this makes all the difference."

"But won't the two situations lead to the same result?" asked Farishta.

"No, they won't. And they cannot. A curious child explores to learn and the parent is there to satisfy her curiosity. But when a parent wrongly perceives a curious child for a naughty child, the child soon learns to be naughty and her natural curious instincts fade away. A naughty child is only interested in the attention she gets for herself and creates disturbance to achieve it. Learning no longer remains her aim. Naughtiness is a learnt behaviour, an adult handout to a child. It is a negative trait which can be destructive at times."

"Then what should parents do to maintain the curiosity of the child and at the same time keep her disciplined?" Farishta was getting curious himself now.

"Parents should answer all the queries of their kids, let them explore and learn, but at the same time teach them that there are limits that have to be kept in mind. Other people's right and property should never be violated. Children should be taught to take permission to explore where other people are involved. For example, when in a friend's house, ask her mother if it is alright to examine something new and interesting. Children should also be taught how to handle a mistake. If they accidentally damage or spill something they should, first of all, own it up, and then try and be of help in cleaning it if the adults feel if is safe for them to do so. Helping in a positive way not only enhances the self-image of the children, it can also be a satisfying learning experience for them."

"Are the parents then responsible for their children being naughty?"

"Yes they are. Absolutely."

"Then why do they never acknowledge their responsibility?"

"Because they do not understand it themselves. You cannot blame the parents also; they do what they think is best according to their own learning. It is only that some of them are not well informed or are not aware of the needs of their children. Or some may not have their own sense of values and worth in the right place. Or they may have their own problems to deal with. Never blame the parents. Their intentions towards their children are seldom wrong. And also never forget that they too are humans and can make mistakes," reasoned Almighty with understanding.

"But can't you teach a child to become disciplined and understanding after she grows up?" Farishta asked with hope.

"No, not really. It is very difficult to change an individual once he or she learns to interpret and perceive things in a certain way and adopts a certain way of life," said Almighty. "Children learn what you teach them; they do not forget it easily after they grow up."

"Then will that little girl always fuss over her food even after she grows up?" Farishta felt concerned.

"In all probability, yes. And she is also likely to expect others to be aware of her requirements in adult life and will want them to fuss over her as well. But this world is not catered to gratify to the needs of any one person and does not pamper anyone the way a parent can. This is precisely why pampered children grow up to be frustrated adults. The worst thing parents can do to their children is to pamper them."

"Then what should a mother do when her child does not eat?"

"Just leave her alone."

"What? Leave a hungry child alone?"

"Yes, that is exactly what she should do. No child ever, and mind you, ever, remains hungry. When the mother does not fuss over the child's food, the child learns to feed herself, without fuss, and stays healthier in the bargain. Most of the mothers today are aware of this simple fact; it is explained in every book. But they choose to ignore this advice instead," said Almighty feeling helpless.

"But why do mothers ignore this advice? Why do they fuss over their children's food when they know that it is not good for them? Why do they not follow the advice given by people who know?" Farishta was totally confused now.

"For roughly the same reasons the little girl gave you. By fussing over her child's food, the mother gets an opportunity to fuss in a camouflaged way. After all, what can be more important than feeding your child?

If the mother is unavailable for her other commitments, so what? Other members of the family are obligated to manage them for her. And that they, in most cases, do.

"With working mothers, the reasons can differ a little. They fuss over their kids also because they feel guilty about leaving them with the ayahs or in the daycare. They try to compensate for it by tempting their kids with goodies, but it seldom works. Like the mother who ordered what she thought her son would like but did not know that he was not interested. Food is seldom as important for a child as it is for the adults. But when food is an issue in the family, it becomes so for the kid as well. This imposed fuss can even teach little children to *hate* some foods that should normally be a delight for them. Like the boy said he *hated* certain flavors of ice-cream. Now tell me, why would a child use such negative terms for something as naturally delightful for a kid as ice-cream? He has obviously learnt it from someone. He hates it just to be fussy.

"You will find a lot of mothers today fussing over their children's food, irrespective of the fact that books and counsellors are telling them not to. It has also become a sort of fashion statement with mothers to try and tell others how busy they are with their kids and how much they do for them," explained Almighty, sounding a little unhappy.

"People never listen to what they do not want to, and finding an excuse is always easy," agreed Farishta. "But do the mothers not care enough for their children to take professional advice more seriously?" he asked.

"They care about themselves enough to ignore that advice and are happy in their own ways. Never forget that people do what they want and no one can make them see reason if they do not want to see it," sighed Almighty and continued-

"Fussing over the kids' food has indeed become the norm these days. Every mother tries to out-do the other mother in the amount of time she gives to looking after her children's needs and how her children give her so much trouble, how naughty they are and what sacrifices she is making for them. Working mothers, because of their added sense of guilt about leaving their children in the care of the ayahs, try to pamper them when they come home and fussing over their food comes in handy. The mothers fuss over their children's food for so many reasons of their own that no amount of counselling helps. How can it? The counsellor does not address the needs of the mother and the problem persists. But again, in most of the cases, the mother herself is not aware of the problem."

"And what about the father? What role does he have in all of this?" Farishta wanted to know.

"You are right, fathers should play an important role in bringing up their children and they should devote as much time to the kids as they can. Some fathers do it and that is very good for the kids. Fathers also tend to take professional advice a little more seriously. But in most cases, and for natural reasons, you will find that it is the mother who has more contact with the kids and hence her role becomes more important," said Almighty.

Farishta was beginning to understand this complex situation a little better now. He decided to call it a day and reflect on what he had learnt. He would see Almighty tomorrow, after his next visit to the earth. He bid farewell to Almighty for the night, thanked him, and left.

THE DEMANDING AND THE DEFIANT CHILD

Farishta was fresh and excited when he woke up the next morning. He had not forgotten his previous day's revelations and was now curious to know more. He wanted to know how little children learn to do what they do. What makes them disobedient and demanding, rude and uncaring, defiant and out of control? After all, no parent can feel good when a child misbehaves or is rude. Even when the parents are rude and demanding themselves, they still want their children to be polite and understanding.

With the rising of the sun, Farishta flew down to earth. Dew was still fresh on the plants and the lawns were sprinkled with pearls. The freshness of the day was simply enchanting.

Little children were out on the streets, waiting for their school buses. They wore colorful clothes and carried their little school bags on their to-be-robust shoulders. Older kids were in their school uniforms. Some had their parents accompanying them while some were left in the care of the other parents. It was a lovely day, so full of life and sparkle. Farishta felt happy to be around.

Farishta saw a group of little kids standing in a queue waiting for their school bus. Their parents stood by their side, enjoying the morning breeze.

A cute little boy was trying to push his way to the front. He demanded that he be allowed to stand first. He was pulling at the little girl in front of him in an effort to push her out of the queue. The little boy's mother stood by his side, indifferent to her child's behaviour. The mother was busy chatting with the other parents and made no attempt to stop her son from harassing the other kid. The little girl was struggling to hold her place; her mother was also not there with her today. She had left her little daughter in the care of the boy's mother, to be put safely on the bus.

When Farishta could stand it no longer, he walked up to the boy's mother and asked, "Should you not stop your son from harassing the little girl in front of him?"

"Oh! That is okay," said the mother dismissing Farishta and his objection.

"But your son is troubling the little girl and trying to encroach upon her space," Farishta protested.

"Oh really?" mocked the mother. "Children have to learn to survive and get what they want. This is a difficult world and you have to learn to fight for yourself," she said.

"But you will not want your son to grab someone else's place, I am sure. Look how he is trying to push the little girl out," Farishta stood his protest and his objection.

"If the girl cannot manage to hold her position, then she has to suffer," the mother shrugged her shoulders and her responsibility.

Farishta was aghast; he did not know what to say. What sort of values are these? Do parents themselves approve of such behaviour, or is this an exception? Farishta found it difficult to believe his eyes and ears. He decided to go around and see what the other children were up to.

He came across a child who was being driven to school by his chauffeur. His mother sat by his side. The little boy was hitting the driver on his head demanding to be taken back home. His mother instructed the driver to ignore the child and keep driving. She made no attempt to stop her child from behaving so.

"Stop the car, I don't want to go to school," protested the little one.

"I will give you chocolates when you come back home," enticed the mother.

"No, I don't want any chocolates," the little one rejected the offer. "I want to go home. I want to play on my computer and watch *Spiderman*," he said pulling the cap off the chauffeur's head. He threw it out of the window.

"Oh, you naughty boy, you must not do such things," chided the mother, patting her little one on his cheek. "I will get you another cap," she assured the driver and off they drove to school.

Before Farishta could understand what such parental attitude could lead to, he saw another child, about three years old, being driven to her prep-school by her father. The mother sat at the back trying to hold her little daughter from crossing over to the front. The little girl was giving her mother a tough time; she wanted to sit in her father's lap, hold the wheel and drive the car with him.

"Sit still, you cannot go to Daddy right now. He is driving and the road is busy," said the mother trying to hold the girl from crossing over.

"No, you leave me," wailed the little one struggling to get out of her mother's grip, "I want to drive with Daddy."

"No you can't," said the father. "There is a lot of traffic on the road and it will disturb me. I will take you for a ride in the colony when I come back in the evening," he assured the child.

"No, I want to drive with Daddy, *now*," howled the little one with all her might.

"Why don't you take her? There is no cop on the road, nothing will happen," was the mother pleading her daughter's case. Holding the girl was a struggle; it was getting on her nerves. She let the girl loose.

The little one promptly crossed over to the front and jumped into her father's lap.

"You are spoiling her; no other child behaves like this. And you also know that it is not safe," said the father as he drove the car with the girl now smiling and holding the wheel with him.

Farishta could not believe his eyes and his ears. How can parents allow such risky behaviour? And, what message was this little girl getting? That you can get what you want, here and now, even if it is risky for you and the others? That it is okay for you to ignore the law; nothing will happen?

Before Farishta could decide what to make out of it, he came across another child telling her mother that she did not want to take her packed lunch to school. She did not like what her mother was giving her.

"I am not taking this lunch to school," she declared. "I do not like these stupid sandwiches you have made for me and you do not listen." She protested, stamping her feet.

"Sorry dear, tomorrow I will give you what you want but take these sandwiches today. You know you were not well yesterday and you need to take home-cooked food," the mother reasoned.

"No I am not taking these sandwiches, and that is final," the girl put her foot down.

"Tomorrow I will give you what you like, I promise," assured the mother.

"No I never like what you give me," dismissed the little one, "I want pizza from Pizza Hut tomorrow," she declared.

"Okay, as you wish. But take these sandwiches today, p-l-e-a-s-e," pleaded the mother.

"No, no way, never. Give me money for the school restaurant instead," she commanded, and the mother obeyed. She was in a hurry to get ready for her office.

The mother went to the father and complained, "Did you see how your daughter just refuses to listen to me?"

"You know that she never listens to anyone, always does the exact opposite of what we tell her to do. Why did you have to say anything to her at all?" the father put the blame on the mother.

"You have spoilt her so," the mother accused.

"Okay, okay, it is all my fault. You let her be. She is my daughter and I can take care of her if you cannot. Just let her do what she wants." The father retorted as the mother stomped away.

And the girl left for school with a smile. She was feeling triumphant and happy.

Farishta was stunned. How can parents allow their children to behave like this? Do they not know that it is not good for them to be so demanding, defiant, and rude? Besides, how will this child learn to be responsible for her own health and well-being? Can such children ever grow up to become responsible and mature adults? Why do parents give in to their children so easily? And why do they accept defiance as the done thing? Are they not spoiling their own kids?

Farishta remembered what Graydon G. Goss has said, "Kids misbehave because parents don't make them behave." And now he was beginning to understand how.

Farishta had a lot of questions coming but, he did not know whom to ask. He would ask Almighty when he got back, but he wanted to hear something from the people here too. He wanted to know what they thought and what they were up to. After all, it is they who are bringing up their kids this way.

He saw an old man out on his morning walk. Farishta walked up to him and greeted him with a smile. The old man looked pleased and acknowledged his greetings. Farishta told him the purpose of his visit and who he was. He also told him how amazed he was at what he had just seen.

The old man shook his head and said, "I too do not understand the new generation at all. Parents have a very different way of looking at things these days. The children are not to be blamed, they only do what their parents let them do or expect them to do. People these days feel that children should be allowed to dictate what they want. They do not believe in restrictions and discipline; they feel it will hamper the growth of their kids."

"But children do need parental guidance to grow up properly," opinioned Farishta. "They need to be disciplined and taught to know the difference between right and wrong, or else how will they know? Besides, research shows that children do like certain limits; it makes them feel secure and cared for," he added.

"You are right," said the old man, "but the parents of little kids mostly feel that if you discipline your kids, it will restrict their growth and potential and as such children should be allowed to do what they want from the very beginning."

"But don't you think that children need to know the rules before they can be trusted with their judgment? And it is the parents' duty to guide them and help them to make the right decisions and not just give in," said Farishta.

"Absolutely right," agreed the old man. "Children do need to know the difference between a good choice and a bad one before they are allowed to make them.

It is the duty of the parents to help their children in making the right choices, however difficult it may be. Besides, civilization is all about discipline, and the more civil you are, the more discipline you adhere to. Without civil behaviour there will only be 'jungle raj.' But parents do not seem to understand this and I do not understand them," he said.

"Don't unruly kids run the risk of becoming wayward youngsters and immature adults? Will it not come in their way of success and happiness later?" asked Farishta with concern.

"You are right, but young parents do not seem to care for this at all. They feel that discipline comes in the way of success; it inhibits the personality of the kids and robs them of the confidence needed to be successful in this increasingly competitive world," explained the old man.

"But there is a difference in being rude and aggressive like a bully, or having faith in oneself and being firm and clear about one's convictions like most successful people. It is right choice that is needed to be successful and happy in life, and this comes from discipline and hard work," said Farishta.

"I wish parents could understand this," hoped the old man as he walked away.

Farishta stood there all by himself, trying to understand this puzzling situation. He could figure out that allowing the kids to be rude and demanding was a new phenomenon which was not normally encouraged in the earlier days. So what is it that the parents are confused about now? What are they aiming at for their kids?

He walked up to a father who had just put his child on a school bus and was hurrying home. Farishta put the same question to him and the father smiled and replied, "When we were kids, we were told what to do; we were never asked what we wanted. And in most cases, we were also not allowed to have our way. This hampered our growth. See how the other countries have progressed while we are still struggling. You have to be daring and bold to sustain the competition today and we want our children to have no inhibitions."

"But you do not have to be rude and uncaring to be bold and daring. In fact, it is the self-confident and the self-assured who are more polite and courteous, and bold too. They are also disciplined and are able to work hard. They are the ones who grow up to have faith in their own abilities and are more successful and lead happier lives," said Farishta trying his best to make the father understand his point.

"No, I do not believe in imposing discipline on my child. She can learn it later when she grows up," the father dismissed Farishta and his argument and hurried away. He was getting late for his office.

Farishta was shocked with this reply. How could the father not know that it was not easy to change the ways of a child after she grows up to adopt a certain pattern of behaviour? What makes him believe that it will be easier to discipline the child after she grows up? Or is it that he is shirking his responsibility and taking an easier way out? Or, is it that he is ignorant and does not understand the importance of discipline and balance in life? Or, is all this put together the cause of this mess?

Farishta walked up to a park and lay down to reflect upon what he had just seen and heard. The little ones were so cute and lovable. They were thinking kids and were experimenting with the world around them. This is the time when they need to be guided the most. They need help to understand things as they are and as they should be. This is the time when their thinking and reasoning is taking shape for all times to come and will reflect in their future. Proper value system, independence, courage, compassion and cooperation are basic qualities needed for success and happiness in life, and they need to be instilled and nurtured in the early years, this he knew. Farishta dozed off trying to figure out the situation for himself.

It was noon when he woke up, and realizing the time, hastily flew back.

Farishta went straight to see Almighty. He wanted to have a meaningful discussion with Almighty before he got busy. There was so much to ask.

Almighty was pleased to see Farishta. He saw the puzzled look on Farishta's face and knew that he had had more than he could comprehend.

"You seem to have had a busy morning today," smiled Almighty.

"Yes, indeed. I have been to the earth and seen a lot. But the more I see, the more amazed I am and the more questions I have for you," admitted Farishta.

"So you have had an enlightening day today as well, and now you need my help to understand what you saw," said Almighty.

"Yes, that's right. The ways of the world are indeed strange. I do not understand them at all. On the one hand, parents are keen to give their children the best of education and the best of opportunities, and on the other hand, they teach them no rules and values. They do not want to impose any discipline; they feel it will restrict the growth of their kids. I do not understand how they think that unruly kids can ever be more successful and happy in life," said Farishta.

"You are right," said Almighty, "parents do not want to enforce any discipline these days and that is what is worrying me a lot."

"But why are parents so against disciplining their kids?" asked Farishta.

"Enforcing discipline has become outdated in the modern day world. You have seen how parents think that it restricts the child's growth. A caring and disciplined child is wrongly thought to be a submissive child who will not be able to stand up for herself or himself when the time comes. And, as such, the parents are afraid to lay down any rules or limits," explained Almighty.

"But don't the parents know that there is no correlation between being submissive and meek, and being caring and disciplined?" queried Farishta.

"That is the problem; this is where the confusion lies. Parents confuse discipline with restrictive control where no independent thought is allowed which, in effect, restricts all growth. They mistakenly believe that if they discipline their children they will grow up to become passive and compliant, subservient and docile, inactive and timid, and will not be able to face new challenges and opportunities that might come their way. They will not be as successful as they deserve to be. Though the opposite is always true. They do not understand that it is right discipline that promotes faith in oneself and one's capabilities. Discipline is at the base of healthy development and rewarding growth. Disciplined people are the ones who reach greater heights and are more successful. Appropriate guidance along with supportive discipline is what makes a child more confident and self-assured," explained Almighty.

"I only know that it is so but I do not know why it is so," Farishta was truthful.

"The reason is simple. People with right discipline are bold and confident because they have better value systems and are more aware of their strengths and limitations. Discipline helps them to be hardworking and cooperative too. They can work for what they want and are able to get things done which enhances their self-esteem in their own eyes. They are also easy to be with and are more open to reason. They are proactive and are able to work in the interest of all. This makes them more successful and likeable, which instills further confidence in them. Developing all these qualities needs proper guidance and discipline which only parents can provide. And once you have these qualities, you cannot be meek and submissive," said Almighty.

"Now I understand the reason for the confusion in the minds of the parents," Farishta enthused. "They feel that if they do not restrict their children in any way, they will grow up to be more confident and assured. They do not know that unguided and undeserved confidence will only lead to confusion and lack of confidence that is needed for the right kind of success and happiness throughout life. You cannot have inner self-assurance till you are confident of your capabilities, and you cannot be sure of your capabilities till you have worked on them. You cannot run a race till you have put in the right effort."

"You are absolutely right," said Almighty. "This is exactly what is happening in the world today. Children are being unwisely encouraged not to follow rules of any kind in the hope of making them bold and confident. But this is proving to be counter productive. It is not only making them defiant, rude, and uncaring, it is also coming in the way of their growth and potential. This defiant confidence can also lead to risky behaviour with disastrous results," he said and continued,

"Like the parents who allowed their little girl to sit with the father and hold the steering wheel while he was driving, though they knew that it was not only risky, it was also not allowed. Now what message do you think this little girl could have got? That your whims and fancies are supreme and you can indulge in risky behaviour and nothing will happen to you; that you can ignore the law and not listen to any one, not even your father or your mother. And if this girl grows up with this message and lives up to it, she is very likely to get into trouble and the parents will not know whom to blame and what to do. They will blame her school, her friends, and the society, but it will never occur to them that they are themselves to blame." Almighty said, shaking his head in disbelief.

"And I have also found that parents, unwittingly though, encourage their children not to listen to them. Do they not know that when they openly say that their children will defy them – like what that little girl's father said about her not listening to anyone, including the parents, and doing just the opposite of what she had been told to do – will encourage her to do just that? In fact, she will be, bound to defy her parents as children, in most cases, do what they think their parents expect them to do," said Farishta after gaining insight from the past day's expedition.

"Yes, parents do not always behave in a responsible manner. And when they are themselves the defying kind, they expect defiance from their kids too and the idea gets communicated. That is how children learn to be like their parents," explained Almighty with reason.

"And by the time parents realize their mistake, it is already too late. Besides, don't you think that it is the defiant kid who runs a greater risk of doing drugs and falling into wrong company and criminal behaviour as well?" asked Farishta with concern.

"Yes, you are right here too. It is the defiant who run a greater risk of doing all the wrong things for they enjoy doing what they are not expected to do or supposed to do. They like to shock their parents at any cost, even their own. People have always known about it and there is a Chinese proverb that says, 'Rogues differ little. Each began first as a disobedient son.' But people in the modern day world do not care about it, or even understand it.

"Defiant children are also likely to rebel against their parents when they feel neglected and out of control. It gives them a false sense of power. They are also more prone to do drugs and they do them for a number of reasons, from defying their parents, to asking for attention. They may also, at times, do drugs for peer acceptance. The need for peer acceptance gains greater significance when the child has low self esteem and feels neglected at home. And in situations where respect for parents is also low, things become all the more difficult. But parents, very often, do not recognize their role in shaping their children's future and are reluctant to acknowledge it. Parents need to take their responsibility more seriously, but they do not always do so," said Almighty helplessly.

"But why do children not listen to their parents? Why do they not respect them enough and hold their views in high esteem? And why do they, so often, just refuse to do what their parents tell them to do? How can parents yield any influence on their children in such a situation?" Farishta was anxious to know.

"Who do you think is responsible for this?" Almighty quipped.

"I do not know," Farishta was truthful.

"Go down to earth tomorrow and find out for yourself," said Almighty and got up. "We shall discuss it later when you come back," he assured him and left.

Now Farishta had a mission for the morrow as well and he was even more curious this time. The more he went down, the more involved he got with the ways of the world and the more amazed he was. He needed to know so much before he could understand what was going wrong that was causing Almighty so much worry. He decided to leave at dawn the next day and got busy with his work.

DISREGARD FOR PARENTS AND THEIR OPINION

Farishta opened his eyes to the beauty of an infant morning. He stretched himself and jumped out of bed. This was the time of the day he liked best, total peace and tranquil calm. So alive and anticipating; so full of hope and promise.

Farishta remembered his assignment for the day. He needed to find out what it was that made children disrespect their parents? Why do they not want to listen to them? What makes them think that their parents do not know enough? Why do children rebel? And what role parents themselves have in it? After all, how could parents ever teach their children not to respect them and their views?

Farishta hurried with his morning chores and flew down. The sun was bright and the day had just begun. The hustle bustle of the earth was enchanting and he felt happy. People were getting ready to go to work and were racing against time. Young parents were busy getting their children ready for school and getting ready for work themselves. Everyone was in a tearing hurry. It was a new morning and a new day was waiting to start. The grandparents in the families had either taken a back seat or were helping their children and grandchildren in whatever way they could.

"Where is my breakfast?" called out a father to his mother.

"I am bringing it in a minute dear," replied the mother cheerfully as she walked in with hot, stuffed, mouth watering, *gobhi parathas*.

"What? Parathas, at this time? Who wants to have *parathas* so early in the morning? Get me something light," the son objected.

"These are your favorite *parathas,* dear, and I got up early in the morning especially to make them for you. You remembered them yesterday and I wanted to give you a surprise," said the mother with a smile.

"No, I don't want to have *parathas* at this time. Give me my usual egg and toast, and bring it quick," ordered the son, and the mother obeyed. She looked a little unhappy, though; her effort had been wasted.

"Why does Daddy behave like this with Dadi?" asked the little grandson as his mother readied him for school, at leisure. She was in no hurry; she was neither a working mom nor felt the need to help with the house work. What could be more important than looking after the kid? The mom-in-law could take care of the house work at least. After all, she had nothing else to do.

"Because Dadi is so dumb. Why did she have to make *parathas* in the morning? Does she not know that Daddy likes to have eggs and toast?" replied the mother with scorn.

"But he likes *parathas* too. Besides, eggs and toast are so boring," said the thoughtful little grandson.

"Dadi should have asked Daddy before making them in any case," the mother insisted.

"But she wanted to give Daddy a surprise," the little one persisted.

"Now, will you stop it? You do not have to be your Dadi's advocate, do you understand?" the mother snapped and the boy obeyed.

Farishta was amazed. What message was this mother giving to her son? That it was okay to treat your mother like this? Or that a mother was only meant to serve, her sentiments were of no value? Or that compassion for a parent was not acceptable? Farishta did not know what to make out of this. He decided to visit other homes and see what was going on there.

The phone was ringing in a home and the lady of the house answered. It was her sister on the line wanting to leave their father in her care, just for a month. She wanted to go out on a holiday with her family.

"So you want to go out for a month and need to send Papa here during that time," the lady of the house repeated as her husband gestured a frantic 'NO'. 'But it is just a matter of a month,' the wife put the phone on mute and whispered.

"No way," said the hubby, "I do not like the look of the old man, can't tolerate him for a minute. Say no to your sister. Make an excuse," he instructed.

"Then where will *Nanaji* go?" this was the little granddaughter showing concern for her Granddad.

"You keep quiet, this is not your problem," the father shouted, and the girl complied.

"You see taking Papa in will not be possible at all. My in-laws are visiting us during that time and we have no extra room. I am so sorry," the mother made up an excuse and put the phone down.

"But Papa's people are not coming. Why did you lie to *Masi*, Mama?" the little girl put in an innocent query.

"Do not poke your nose when you do not know anything," the father growled, but the little girl was unable to hold her curiosity this time.

"Why does Nanaji always live with *Masi* and not us, Mama? And why does Daddy not like him?" the little girl ignored her father's anger. She was unable to comprehend this mysterious situation and wanted to have an answer.

"Because Daddy does not have patience with him; he finds Nanaji's presence annoying," explained the mother sounding a little guilty.

"But I like him and I want him to come and stay with us for some time, please Mama," the little girl pleaded, expecting to get her wish fulfilled and her Nana's problem solved.

"No, that is not possible," thundered the father. And getting angrier, he continued, "And I do not want to hear another word from you now, do you understand? Finish your breakfast, it is time for you to go to school," he bullied the girl into obedience.

The girl had a lot of questions coming but could not dare to ask. She felt sorry for her Nana; he was such a loveable man. It was a pleasure to have him around and talk to him. He always had time for her and he told her such interesting stories. Her parents never gave her as much attention as her Nana did. Besides, who would look after him when Mausi went out? The girl looked at her mother's face for an answer, but could get nothing. The mother appeared indifferent and unconcerned. The girl knew her Dad did not like his own parents either, and she did not know why.

Farishta was astounded. What were these parents up to and what example were they setting for their child? Do they not know what F. Randolph has said as a timely warning for the parents-'Whoever makes his father's heart to bleed, shall have a child that will revenge the deed.'

Farishta moved on to another home. The father was narrating the tale of his smartness to the mother and she was feeling proud of him. After all he had managed to outsmart his colleagues to obtain his promotion. He had projected the work of his whole team as his own and the trick had worked.

"But Daddy, if you take credit for other people's work will it not amount to cheating?" asked the five-year-old sounding a little confused.

"No, I was a member of that team, it was my work too," said the father, dismissing the query with no feeling of any guilt.

"We should celebrate your promotion this weekend. Let us have a big party. After all you are getting a big raise and everyone in your office will be jealous." This was the mother feeling thrilled with her new-found status and the big opportunity to show off.

Just then the phone rang, "Hello," answered the mother, "let me just see; he was leaving for his office," she told the caller and putting the phone on mute said to the father, "This is your colleague, what should I tell him?" she asked.

"Tell him I have left for office," said the father. And sitting down for his breakfast murmured, "Must be wanting to share the credit with me".

The child looked on with confusion. He did not know what to make out of what he had just witnessed. He looked at his parents for clues, but could see nothing. Were his parents right or was there something wrong about the whole affair? Why did his father not take the phone? Why did he make Mama lie to his colleague and why did he not want to share the credit with him when he was also a part of the same team? There was something strange about the whole affair, he knew. But what could it be? He gulped down his glass of milk and left for school. Still at a loss and with no answers.

Farishta did not know whom to feel sorry for, the parents or the child. The parents had sown a seed of doubt about themselves in the mind of their child and the child was not sure of what to make out of the episode he had just witnessed. His sense of values was starting to take root and he was puzzled. Will he now begin to doubt everything that his parents said or did? Is it possible for a child to respect his parents when he cannot trust them? Will he be able to trust others when he cannot trust his own people? And above all, will he grow up to be trustworthy himself?

Farishta moved to yet another home. The parents there were having a fight. They were busy accusing and blaming each other while the kids watched, looking helpless as they waited for help in getting ready for school.

"Why don't you put your paper down and prepare the lunch boxes while I get the kids ready?" shouted the mother.

"You know I am not good at cooking, let me help the kids instead," the father kept his cool as he folded the morning paper.

"You are good at nothing," the mother snapped, "can't even learn to cook properly. You do what you like, I am not going into the kitchen today," she put her foot down.

"Cooking is not my job; I am not doing it anyway," the father shot back.

"I too go to the office like you, why me?" the mother yelled.

"So what? Stop going to the office if you like. But for God's sake let there be some peace in the house", the father retorted.

"Oh, really? Stay at home, eh. I would love to do that. But how much do you think you earn that I can sit at home and enjoy life like the other wives do?" the mother mocked, and then went on, "Why did you marry if you could not provide for your family?" she screamed.

"What do you mean?" shouted the father. "Who brings money for the family? Do you? So what if you bring in some meager amount? You spend it all on yourself anyway and you think you do me a favour," he roared.

"Yes, I do you a favour by not asking you to meet my expenses. It is your job to provide for the family, including me, do you understand? Do you have your eyes on my money too?" shrieked the mother as she stomped into the kitchen.

"Will you shut up? I have never touched your money and you know that. If you want to be extravagant, you have to provide for it yourself, and that's it," said the father as he got up to help the kids.

Farishta was aghast with this exchange. What message were the kids getting? Is it possible for them to respect either parent when they hear such accusations and insults?

The more Farishta explored the world, the more confusing it became. Things were so straight and simple; your children will learn what they are exposed to. How can they learn anything else? But why were people here not able to understand this natural and inevitable law? It was so obvious and so simple.

Farishta came out on the streets. He wanted to take a walk in the fresh and cool air. He needed time to reflect and understand what he had just seen and heard. Almighty was always there to explain things to him later, but he too wanted to understand them for himself before he asked.

He saw little children out on the streets, waiting for their school buses. Their parents, who had come to drop them, were standing in groups talking and boasting about whatever they could.

"See what a beautiful chart my son made yesterday," said a mother showing the chart she was carrying for her son. "His drawing is so good he-- --"

"You did that for me, Mama," the boy intervened. He was feeling proud of his mother.

"I only helped you a little, you did most of it, isn't it?" replied the mother sounding a little embarrassed. The boy could feel the discomfiture of his mother as he nodded his head in affirmation. A little reluctantly though.

"My daughter wrote a poem about the picnic her class went for the other day. She has to recite it in her class today," another mother was quick to boast in response.

There was a tug at the mother's hand. The little girl wanted to say something. The mother bent down.

"You wrote that poem for me Mama," whispered the little one as softly as she could.

"That does not matter," the mother whispered back.

And Farishta was floored again. Most of the things about this world were beyond him. What was the need for these two mothers to tell lies and boast about their children? Is boasting more important than truth? Those who feel the need to brag the most normally have the least to brag about, he knew. Besides, were they not undermining their kids and finding them inadequate? Or else, why would they try to improve their image with the help of lies? Will these children not learn to feel good by imagined achievements rather than real ones? Will it not come in the way of their success and happiness later on in life? Can a kid respect a parent who cannot be trusted? And above all, did the two mothers believe each other in any case?

Farishta was beginning to understand the dilemma of Almighty now. He has created this world so much like his own place and has given humans the best he could. Almighty has also given them the power of independent thinking and the capability to enjoy the bounty he had bestowed on them, the way they liked. Or even to improve upon it, if they so desired. And they have been partially successful in it too. But they have improved only in the area of science and technology. As far as human qualities go; they are turning it the other way. If the parents mess up raising their kids, then how will they grow up to be conscientious and responsible adults? If people living here are not mature and dependable, caring and compassionate, honest and straightforward, patient and understanding, then how can it feel like heaven? In spite of all its natural bounty and scientific growth.

Farishta felt sorry for Almighty and his people. He remembered what Jacqueline Kennedy Onassis had once said- 'If you bungle raising your children, I don't think whatever else you do well matters very much.' People on earth have been obsessed with Jacqueline for a long time but they do not seem keen to take note of her one sensible and simple advice.

And with a heavy heart Farishta flew back.

Almighty was getting up from his afternoon siesta when Farishta arrived. One look at Farishta's face told him that he had had a revealing and upsetting day. The ways of the world were indeed disturbing, but what could Almighty do? He had placed his confidence in humans and made them to be independent thinking beings who had the affairs of the world in their hands. He had given them perceptive and receptive little kids whom they could bring up the way they liked. They could make them responsible and caring adults, capable of making this world the most beautiful place to be in. It could be heaven on earth in no time. But humans were messing it for sure.

The law of creation is simple, you reap what you sow. But humans, it appears, never seem to understand this natural and simple law of life. They think they are smarter. They want to get the desired results but without putting in the right effort. They do not appear to understand, or even care, what examples they are setting for their kids. And children, we all know, may not listen to their parents but will grow up to be like them for sure.

Bacon has said, so long ago, 'Parents who wish to train up their children in the way they should go, must go in the way they would have their children go.' But parents forget this simple and unquestionable law when it comes to them.

Farishta sat down next to Almighty, "Today It was indeed a disturbing day for me. I had gone down to see what makes kids develop disrespect for their parents and I have seen a lot. I did not know that there is so much insensitivity towards old parents in the world and little children witness it all the time. Besides, parents also tend to, at times, treat each other with disrespect. And they are also not always straightforward and honest in their ways, and children seem to understand it when it is so. All this could be contributing to the disrespect the kids develop for their own parents," he said.

"Yes, grown ups do not always treat their parents well, though I have made little children revere their parents to start with. This helps them to learn at the fast pace that they need to. In the beginning, children treat every word their parents say as the only truth and are ready to learn from them without question. But humans, I find, are failing to make proper use of this opportunity that I have given them. They do not take care to be the right examples for their kids. When little children see their parents disrespecting their own parents they too learn to disrespect their parents in the process. They learn it as the done thing. What else can it be?" said Almighty.

"You are right. The parents I saw today were totally indifferent to the needs of their own parents and the kids seemed to understand it. I was myself amazed at their behaviour," said Farishta. "Another problem that I have seen today is that parents are not always straightforward and honest in their own dealings and children notice all that. They start doubting their parents and their motives. And this adds to the problem," said Farishta with concern.

"You are right. Children understand things as they are, for they do not filter information according to their own beliefs; their minds are fresh and receptive, and without any prejudice or preconceived notions. This helps them to have a keener perception and better understanding than what adults think they have. Children cannot be fooled into believing what is not true. As they are new to the world they see everything as it is, and they learn fast. They do not modify anything to suit their own opinion or way of life.

"Leo Tolstoy has been wise enough to observe- 'Hypocrisy may deceive the cleverest man, but the least wide-awake of children recognizes it.' But parents think otherwise. They think children can be fooled into believing what is not true," said Almighty shaking his head in disbelief and continued,

"Without this extraordinary ability to understand things, it would not be possible for children to learn so much and so fast. Children take everything at face value to start with, and do not doubt the intentions of the adults in their lives, especially their own parents. And as such, they learn more from them than anyone else. But parents are messing it all up," he said.

"That is what I could also gather from my visits to the earth," said Farishta. "But I can't understand how parents do not understand this," he said with surprise.

"When the adults in the lives of the kids are not reasonable and mature, caring and giving, tolerant and helpful, then what can the kids learn from them? Difficult parents have difficult kids. And when they pamper their kids they become selfish and demanding as well, further adding to the problem. I have made parents the most influential people in the lives of the kids, they are their role models. But children, after they grow up, will listen to their parents only when they respect them enough. Parents need to set proper example for their kids to help them grow into responsible adults," he said.

"And to top it all, they also slight each other in front of the kids and the kids are then bound to develop disrespect for them both," added Farishta.

"Yes, that is right. You cannot insult each other and then expect your child to respect either of you for that," said Almighty.

"What should the parents do to ensure that their kids develop proper respect for them?" asked Farishta.

"To be able to command respect from their children, parents have to be respect-able themselves. They have to be mature and reasonable, caring and giving, honest and straightforward, where they do not have to hide or justify anything that they do or say. They have to be what they want their kids to be.

"Parents should understand that kids are not mature enough to deal with bickering between them and they should not try to resolve their differences while children are around. Belittling each other in front of the kids will only make the kids insecure and disrespectful of both. Parents should never try to gain sympathy of their kids in any way. The kids are smart enough to understand it and it will rebound on the parent sooner or later," said Almighty.

"Now I can understand what the problem is and what needs to be done," Farishta said with hope. "First of all, parents need to be straightforward and honest themselves, they have to be respectful towards their own parents for the kids learn from what they see. And the parents also have to respect each other and be caring and mature in their ways. In short, parents will command respect of their kids when they deserve it right," said Farishta.

"Absolutely correct. You will also find very fine people out there in the world and their children know it. These children are proud of their parents and they are always keen to listen to them and take their advice at any stage and in any sphere. But they are few and far between," said Almighty sounding a little unhappy, and added,

"And the problem has a wider consequence than what people think. When kids do not respect their parents, they have no proper guiding force in their lives. They become rebellious and insecure and are then at the mercy of the forces of the outside world around them. It then becomes easy for them to fall victim to the wrong influences from where the parents, having lost the trust of their kids, may not always be able to save them.

"I hope parents understand this and do their best to be the right models for their kids. It is so simple and straightforward. Parents just have to have their values in the right place. And I hope they will soon learn to," Farishta tried to be optimistic.

"I am waiting for that day," said Almighty as he got up. "Take another round of the earth tomorrow and let me know what you see," he said.

Farishta thanked Almighty and took his leave. He was feeling tired and needed rest. The day had been more revealing and taxing than he had thought.

JEALOUSY AND SIBLING RIVALRY

Next day, the sun was already up by the time Farishta opened his eyes. It was another beautiful morning and he had missed out on the magnificence of daybreak and the tranquil peace of the first morning rays.

Anyway, the day was still beginning and he could go down and see a lot. Farishta jumped out of bed, looking forward to his next round of the earth. Today he wanted to know what made children develop strong emotions of jealousy and hatred. What made them rivals of their own siblings, their own flesh and blood, people who were so near and dear to them? The very people they are supposed to nurture and care for, love and protect and feel secure and happy with. Siblings are neither buyable nor replaceable and are the most precious gift bestowed by the Almighty. Humans should be thankful to him for that.

Farishta hurried with his morning chores at double speed and sailed down to earth. His earlier visits had been astonishing and revealing; he now wanted to learn more and understand better. The more he found out about the ways of the world, the more involved he got, and the more amazed he was.

As Farishta descended on the earth, he saw merrymaking in a home. A new baby had arrived and people were celebrating her birth. Farishta peeped into the nursery and saw a cute little newborn wrapped in a pink blanket. The baby was sleeping peacefully while her little big brother, about four years old, stood by her side keeping vigil and feeling proud and happy with his new-found status and the new addition to his family.

The boy looked up at Farishta and smiled, "See what a fantastic little sister God has sent me."

"Oh yes, she is indeed precious and adorable. I am so happy for you," said Farishta patting the little brother on his cheek. He then bent down to have a closer look at the newborn.

"Shish-s-s, be careful, do not touch her or else she might wake up and cry," whispered the little big brother as softly as he could. "She is so small and delicate, we have to look after her and not disturb her," he said. He understood the responsibility of a big brother, and Farishta was impressed. How caring and considerate this little one was! He was looking after his baby sister while the nanny was away. A new born should not be left unattended, he knew, especially when so many guests were coming in to have a look at her.

Just then, the nanny opened the door and the baby stirred. The little brother stretched his hand and gently patted the baby in an attempt to sooth her, but the nanny thought otherwise. She pulled the boy aside and said, "Do not disturb the baby, you naughty boy, or I will have to tell your parents," she admonished.

"I am not disturbing the baby; I am looking after her," the brother retorted as the father entered the room, and hearing what the nanny had just said, he too was quick to reprimand the boy.

"If you disturb your little sister, you will be sorry," he warned.

"But I am not disturbing her; I am looking after her," the little one stood his ground and his protest.

"I know you well, you naughty boy. Do not try to be smart with me," the father snapped, and ignoring the boy now, he gently smiled and touched the new born on her cheeks. The father looked pleased and happy as the little brother looked on, a little unhappy this time. He was feeling wronged.

"Do not let him be alone with the baby," the father instructed the nanny as he left the room.

Farishta was stunned. The little boy had been humiliated and scolded for no fault of his and now the father did not want to trust him with the baby either. The boy had, in fact, been scolded for being caring and responsible. Both the nanny and the father had not even bothered to know what he was doing and what he had to say. What would have happened had the little baby started to cry? After all, that is the only way in which babies communicate. Would the boy have been held responsible for that too, and so unfairly?

Farishta was too shocked to react. What could he say to the little boy or the people who had wronged him so? Was the excitement of the new baby blinding them to the needs of their older child? How could that be so? He decided to visit more homes and see what was happening there. Almighty was always there to explain things to him later.

He saw two little boys playing in their garden while their mother sat there reading a book. The kids appeared to be about two and four years old, respectively. They were having fun kicking a big ball and chasing each other around when their grandmother walked in. The grandmother was happy to see the kids and picking the younger one up, she showered him with kisses and gave him the remote toy car she had brought for the boys. The kids were pleased to see their grandmother too. The older boy came running and hugged his granny; he wrapped his hands round her waist.

The grandmother looked down at the boy and smiled, "So you want to be picked up too?"

"Oh, he is always like that. Whenever I pick up the younger one he comes running, he is so jealous of his kid brother, you know," joined in the mother as she got up from her chair.

The grandmother put the younger one down and lifted the older kid up. She could not lift both of them together. The younger one protested at first, and then, looking at his new toy, decided to play with it instead.

Now the older kid wanted to be put down too. The new car appeared to be so interesting. He promptly snatched the car from his brother and switched it on, the car zoomed into action. Now the little one wanted the control of the car too but the big brother would not give it to him. He was too small for it, he said. But the younger one just refused to let in. He howled and thrashed and tried to snatch the control but the older kid would not let go, he had an edge. The scuffle turned into a riot in no time. Both the mother and the grandmother tried to intervene, but the kids just refused to listen. Soon the ruckus was beyond their control.

"This is an everyday problem," said the mother, "they create such a racket over every thing that I always have to get two things at a time. They are extremely jealous of each other and are so possessive of their things that they are never willing to share." She complained showing her helplessness and shrugging her responsibility.

"I should have done that too, got two cars, but somehow I forgot," admitted the grandmother feeling responsible and guilty for the hullabaloo in the house. "In future I will also get two things for them," she resolved.

Farishta did not know what to make out of this, who was responsible and how the situation ought to have been handled? Was this jealousy or simple curiosity? And the adults were interpreting it in their own way. He remembered what the psychologists have been saying for a long time, 'you see in others what you have in you'. Were the mother and the grandmother seeing too much? Farishta decided to visit a few more homes and see how things were with them.

He came across two little brothers, about five and six years old, quarrelling over a pencil they had both taken a fancy to. They were hitting each other in a bid to snatch it from the other.

Their father, who could bear the commotion no longer, reprimanded, "Aren't you both ashamed of yourselves, fighting over a pencil?"

"What else will they fight over at this age? Property?" This was the mother's rejoinder to the father's anger.

And the father kept quiet.

Farishta was aghast; did the mother not know what message this statement could carry for her kids? Was she not, in a way, telling them that it was okay for brothers to fight? Or indeed, that it was even expected of them to do so? That there was always something you could fight over at any age. Farishta was not sure. He would find out from Almighty when he got back, and he moved on.

He came across a girl, about eight years old, stamping her feet in anger. Her mother looked on and smiled. The girl would not let her mother pack food packets for her younger sister's school trip. After all, she had not done so for the girl when she had gone on a similar trip the year before. The school was to provide everything, the mother knew. The extra needs of the kids on a train journey had escaped her attention and the girl had to share what her friends had brought, at their mercy. She was furious with her mother when she got back but it was too late then.

The mother was now taking care not to repeat the same mistake a second time, but the girl would not let her. She was demanding that her sister too should not get what was not given to her. And the mother was amused with the *childlike* behavior of her daughter. (How typical of a parent it was.) She was enticing the girl with gifts in an effort to make it up for her but the girl was being difficult; she wanted to extract a good price. Then finally, a deal was struck. Tomorrow, after the sister's departure, both the mother and the daughter would first go to 'Essel World' and then buy a new doll for the girl and whatever else she wanted.

Farishta was flabbergasted, reward for objectionable behaviour? Will this not reinforce rivalry among the sisters and make them more selfish and demanding as well? Was the mother not supposed to talk to the girl and make her understand how she was, in fact, expected to remind her not to make the same mistake again? Should the girl's experience not help her sister? Is this expecting too much from a sibling? Farishta did not know.

It was enough for the day and Farishta decided and started on his way back, but before he could take off he saw a huge crowd gathered at the gate of a hospital. Some prominent person had just died and people were mourning his death. Farishta went closer and enquired, "What is the matter, who has passed away?"

"Oh, he was a great man, an outstanding leader of our country and our party. He had a great future ahead and we expected a lot from him. He was from our young brigade and his tragic and untimely death is an irreparable loss to us and the nation," grieved a mourner.

"Oh! I am so sorry hear that. But how did the young man die? Did he meet with an accident or something?" asked Farishta with concern.

"No, his brother killed him."

"What? What did you say? His brother killed him? His own kith and kin killed him? How can that be possible? And why?" Farishta asked with disbelief.

"Yes, that is right, his own brother did it. Out of jealousy. This brother is an unsuccessful man and could not tolerate the phenomenal rise of his big brother, though his brother always helped him and came to his rescue whenever needed. And now, not only is he denying all that his brother ever did for him, he is also claiming that his brother used to insult him and treat him badly," said the man shaking his head in disgust.

And Farishta was stumped again. The ways of the world were indeed strange and totally out of his comprehension. How could a sibling hate the other so, especially when he was always taking advantage of him? Today's revelations made him sad and unhappy and he wanted to call it a day. He now needed to go back and talk to Almighty; this was getting too much for him. And he hastily flew back.

Almighty was pleased to see Farishta. He knew about Farishta's mission for the day and knew it would be tough for him. He expected him to come back totally shocked and with a lot of unanswered questions. And that is exactly how it turned out to be.

"I am really bowled over today, especially with the last incident I saw," said Farishta.

"Yes, it is indeed lamentable, siblings becoming enemies," agreed Almighty, "and the most tragic part is that this emotion of jealousy and hatred would never have taken root, and, in any case, would never have become so strong had it been handled properly by the adults in the lives of the children when they were small," he said.

"Do you mean to say that parents have a role in this too?" Farishta was shocked. "But how can that be possible?" he was finding it difficult to believe his ears.

"Yes, that is right. Most of the parents, very wrongly though, believe that sibling rivalry is natural and inevitable, and, as such, they unknowingly encourage it in many indirect and subtle ways. They think that jealously is an inborn trait that has to be either accepted, or ignored, or punished, as the case may be. But this is not really so. What is natural is a spirit of healthy competition, not rivalry. And in no case enmity of any kind. Ever.

"Did you notice how parents presume their children will be jealous of each other and unwittingly suggest it to them all the time? The little boy was not jealous of his new sister today, but with this attitude of the adults in his life, he will soon learn to be. You saw how he was taking care of his little sister with concern, but the adults interpreted his behaviour otherwise, according to their own long-held beliefs, and the boy is very likely to pick it up soon.

"And the mother and the grandmother of the two little boys were themselves interpreting their children to be rivals and jealous of each other, even though the kids were happily playing before the new car came. Their natural curiosity for the new toy was misinterpreted by the adults as rivalry. The expectations of the parents always get communicated to the children and they, very understandably, learn to live up to them.

"And of course, you also noticed how the utterance of the mother of the two older boys was suggestive of rivalry between brothers being normal, or rather expected. A mother's opinion is very important for a kid. He thinks that she is the do all and know all, and is right all the time. And a child always aspires to come up to the expectations of the mother. Whether it is negative or positive is irrelevant.

"The third mother was directly rewarding negative behaviour. Instead of reprimanding her older child for not letting her pack food packets for her younger sister's school trip and making her realize that it was, in fact, her duty to remind her mother to do so, she was rewarding her objectionable behaviour. The mother seemed to take sibling rivalry as the done thing and totally natural, unavoidable, and acceptable, and was amused by it as well. She was thus unwittingly encouraging it in her own way. What do you think can come out of such parental attitude? And who do you think teaches siblings to be rivals in such cases?" asked Almighty with concern.

"Now I understand it a little better", said Farishta. "Parents do seem to believe that sibling rivalry is inevitable and natural and their belief gets conveyed to their kids. It also appears to me that they do not really know what they are teaching their kids through their inappropriate and insensitive response to normal everyday life situations. I was myself amazed at what I saw today", he said.

"Parents are not always mindful of what they do and say and that is a big problem," said Almighty. "They rarely have any idea of what goes into the tender minds of their kids, how much they can understand, how important their utterances are and what messages they could convey. Parents perceive and interpret everything according to their own expectations and belief systems. They unknowingly and unwittingly pass it on to their kids," he explained.

"But I also thought that some sibling rivalry was inevitable and natural. So much has been written and said about it that it should be normal and acceptable. Even some psychologists believe that it is so I am told," said Farishta.

"Yes, there is a lot of confusion here. As I have told you earlier, what is natural and normal is a healthy spirit of competition where a child wants to perform better than her siblings, or the other people around her, and likes to contribute more and be well thought of. Every child, when allowed to, will prefer to derive satisfaction out of positive behaviour. It is only when she is not allowed to, or is not able to make a positive contribution will she turn to negative satisfaction. Negative rivalry is an adult hand-out to the kids, which, when suggested to them again and again, they grow up to believe in. And then enact it in their lives as expected and natural. They then pass it on to the next generation and the cycle goes on.

"But you will find that wherever the parents are careful about what they say and expect from their kids, the spirit of competition does not take an ugly turn and siblings remain best of friends throughout their lives," continued Almighty. "They do not hesitate to make any sacrifice for their brothers and sisters and are always a pillar of strength for one another. But that is so rare to come by these days," he said shaking his head with a sigh.

"Then what should the parents do to ensure that their kids do not become rivals and jealousy does not creep in between them?" asked Farishta.

"First of all, they should not presume that their kids will be jealous of each other. Because when you expect something, you unknowingly let the message go. This is exactly what was happening in the homes you visited today.

"Next, prepare the older child to receive the new baby willingly, without feeling threatened, or *dethroned,* as is known in popular jargon today. Give her the confidence that she can never be displaced for she has her own place in the family which no one can take away from her. Ever. Make her understand that as the new baby will be much smaller and more dependent, she will need more attention, and that is all.

"Where the older child is not old enough to understand all this, the parents should take care not to let her feel neglected. It is natural for a very young child to come running to the mother when she picks up the younger sibling or another child. As had happened with the two little brothers you saw. According to the laws of nature, a small child, not being able to look after herself, needs assurance from the mother or the caregiver that she will not be abandoned. When she gets that assurance, she will be satisfied. Do not interpret this natural need of a child to be jealousy," explained Almighty, "and it will not turn into it," he added. "Besides, always take care not to compare any two children. Always keep in mind that no two children are alike; they have their own requirements and their own pace of growth and learning. Respect their individualities and you will not have rivals in your family," he said.

Now Farishta was beginning to understand what was happening in the world. He had seen it for himself today. But he could still not understand how a brother could grow up to hate a brother enough so as to kill him.

Farishta asked Almighty to explain this baffling situation more explicitly and Almighty obliged.

"If a child grows up in a negatively charged and resentful environment, what can you expect from him? Can he learn to be grateful and thankful?" asked Almighty.

"Very unlikely," admitted Farishta.

"And what will happen if you brand him as the angry young man of the family, reward him for his tantrums, do not appreciate good qualities of others in front of him lest he feels threatened, and always bow down to his unjust demands?" asked Almighty and Farishta started to understand what could have happened in the lives of these two brothers. (You can only make a general guess unless you know them closely.) The family must have, unwittingly though, branded one as the responsible and productive member of the family while the other one could have been branded as the angry and irresponsible one. And children, in most cases, live up to play the roles their families assign them.

There could also be both positive and negative role models in the family who could have exercised their influence on the two brothers till they formed their own pattern of life and started to live it. Teaching children to manage their anger constructively is also very important. Whenever the family fails to do so, unfortunate consequences follow.

Today's revelation made Farishta as anxious about the future of the children as Almighty was. After all, harmonious relations in a family are of utmost importance and that is what is most lacking in the world today. Siblings are the most precious gift God has bestowed on mankind, but mankind is somehow unable to enjoy and appreciate it. It is indeed a pity that siblings turn into rivals. And nothing can be more appalling and inexcusable when they turn into enemies.

Farishta thanked Almighty and took his leave. The events and revelations of the day had saddened him and he needed to relax and unwind. He decided to go down for another revealing and exhaustive trip the next day, and left.

He now wanted to know what other influences played their role in shaping the personalities of the kids. What is it, besides parental inputs that is influencing the beliefs and perceptions of the children and making this world so selfish and insensitive? Why is there so much violence in the world today? And how could the parents be unknowingly responsible for that too?

THE ROLE OF ELECTRONIC MEDIA

Farishta lazed around in the morning the next day. He was in no hurry to go down to the earth; he had decided to go down later, after the kids came back from school. He wanted to see how they spent their day at home and what they did. What other things, besides the examples set by their parents were affecting their personalities and why. And what role parents had in it.

Farishta tidied up his place and enjoyed a leisurely breakfast. He came out into his garden and sat under a tree to savour the bounty of nature and the tranquil calm of the morning at home. Everything around him was so beautiful and serene and he felt happy. Farishta reflected upon his visits to the earth in these past few days and realized that the earth was no less beautiful and bountiful than his world here. It is astonishing how Almighty has been so generous in creating this plentiful planet to spectacular perfection. Such a beautiful planet in this largely uninhabitable universe! Amazing. Almighty has been exceptionally partial to his very special creation, the humans. But are they able to enjoy this gift? Thinking of this made him sad.

Humans are messing up with all that they have been given. Besides having a beautiful planet to live in, they also have a thinking and creative brain which they can use to their benefit and live as happy and peaceful a life as they like. When nurtured and brought up well, children can be their main source of joy and happiness, providing meaning and continuity to their lives. Every living species has young ones but they do not have a compassionate mind and that makes all the difference. Love, affection, kindness, gentleness, sympathy, thoughtfulness, concern, understanding, consideration, selflessness, care of the weak and the infirm, and the like, are all human qualities that are not to be seen elsewhere. In the sphere of nature, it is basically just the survival of the fittest and nothing else. There are no emotions and thought involved and the modern-day human is fast reverting to this stage, leaving all human qualities behind. They are fast getting into the rat-race of unhealthy competition and unnecessary acquisitions. How can these unhealthy traits provide happiness and satisfaction they are looking for? Just imagine, if the whole world belonged to you but you had no one to call your own, no one for you to care for, and no one who would care for you, how would it be then?

As Farishta sat there reflecting on his thoughts, the Sun rose to its full strength. Realizing the time, he flew down. It was noon and time for the little kids to return home from their schools. Their mothers, ayahs, or an adult member of the family were at the bus stops waiting to escort them home.

The buses arrived and the little ones jumped out, cheerful and happy. Some handed their bags to the adults, while some carried them themselves and sprinted home. It was a beautiful sight to see the little ones merrily trot home after a good day at school.

A boy asked his mother, "Have you got my '*Mightyman*' DVD today, Mama?"

"Yes dear, I have," the mother replied and the boy jumped with glee. His little sister too was happy with the news and they started to run home; their mother followed them as fast as she could. The moment they reached home, the kids switched on the TV and sat down to watch the DVD their mother had brought and were soon immersed in the program, while their mother fixed their meal. She had taken special care to cook their favourite dishes today; after all, she was a very loving and caring Mom and could do anything to make her kids happy. She called out to them to come and have their meal, but they would not budge. The program was so interesting.

The kids had their meal watching the DVD and were unable to give attention to what they ate. This disappointed their mother a little but she was an understanding Mom. She was happy to see her kids enjoying the program and did not disturb them. There was a lot of action on the screen and the kids were transfixed. They had watched this DVD at a friend's home the other day and its captivating effect had impressed their mother and she brought it for them. Making her kids happy was her first priority. And then, this would also give her time for her much-needed afternoon nap.

Farishta noticed that action meant violence too. He did not know if it was ok for little kids to watch so much cruelty. What message were they getting from it? Will it not affect their tender minds? Can it make them less sensitive to brutality later in life?

Farishta went to another home. The kids there were busy watching a cartoon movie on TV and were refusing to eat anything. Their mother was sitting with their food, making them eat one morsel at a time.

After some time of coaxing the kids to eat something, the mother got tired and left. She too wanted to watch her afternoon programs on the other TV in her room. This TV was working as a babysitter for the kids and she was happy and satisfied.

This was a good way of keeping the kids entertained while the mothers did what they wanted. Some kids' program did not have any violence or negative message and should be okay, thought Farishta though he knew that TV was not recommended for little kids. But what was the harm in watching harmless programs? He would have to ask Almighty. He moved on to another home to see what was going on there.

The adults in the house were watching a movie on the TV in the living room while the kids played around. As usual, it was a movie with a lot of negative roles not suitable for the tender minds of the kids; it was full of substance abuse and sex as well. But the adults in the house did not seem to mind. Kids are exposed to all sorts of things in the world, so what was the harm? Besides, how could little kids understand all this?

But can the kids really not understand what they see? Will it not leave an impression on their tender minds even if they do not understand it right now? And is there no difference in getting a wrong message from the outside world or getting it in your own home, amongst your own people? Will watching a negative role with their own family not endorse it for them more fully? The world out there is virtually the same for every child, but it does not affect them in the same way, this Farishta knew. Different kids choose different company and make different choices. What role does their family and environment have in it, he wondered.

Farishta peeped into another home and found the kids busy playing video games on their computer while the nanny sat there reading a book. These days kids as old as three have a computer of their own. These computers serve a double purpose; they keep the kids busy and allow the adults to do their work uninterrupted. The nanny had been instructed not to let the kids watch too much TV, just about an hour or so, and she took care to do just that. As the kids wanted to watch a kids' program that would be telecast an hour later they were playing video games now.

Farishta went to have a closer look at the game. It was a fight between the police and the bandits and there was a lot of shooting involved. The more number of bandits you shot, the more you scored. And the shooting scenes were explicit, with blood and all. The makers of the games had taken pains to make them as real as possible. Farishta was not sure how harmless it was for the young minds.

In one home, he chanced upon a welcome sight. The mother was playing with her kids and was involved with them. They were reading stories together and making drawings. Not only were they enjoying the afternoon, they also appeared to have a close and caring bond. It was a beautiful sight, so different from the others he had just witnessed. He knew that children needed adult guidance and company for proper growth and development. This is the time when they develop their skills and creative instincts for future and play is the best way to do it, this also he knew. Play gives kids not only an opportunity to be creative and imaginative; it teaches them how to interact with others and be patient and understanding, to take turns and obey rules. The way the brain is used causes it to develop accordingly. Even the physical structure of the brain gets affected by what it is exposed to early in life. Those kids who are exposed to music as little infants develop more brain cells in the auditory area of the brain.

In one home he saw another rare sight and was impressed. The kids were helping their mother with her work and they were all enjoying doing it. The mother was being extra patient with her kids as the little ones were taking time helping her, but they seemed to enjoy working together and looked happy and satisfied with themselves. It was giving the little ones a feeling of being important and useful members of their family and the mother did not want to deprive them of the satisfaction by finishing her work herself. Though that would have been faster and easier for her.

Farishta knew that people who did meaningful work as kids are, in general, more successful and happy in life. And the sooner they start, the better it is; even as early as two years when the toddler can pick up her toys and put them away at the right place. But how and why it works, he would have to ask Almighty, he thought.

The little ones in these two homes definitely looked more satisfied and happy and the adults were also enjoying being with them. Farishta knew that humans are the best toys kids can have. Kids can leave all their toys behind when invited by the adults to play with them. He could also make out that interacting with adults was a very satisfying learning experience for the kids.

It is not that in the other homes the adults did not care for the kids; the only difference was that the kids were left to themselves to enjoy their day as they liked and they were also busy in activities that did not need active participation from them. TV came in handy as an entertainer, virtually working as a baby sitter, and the adults were happy. Even while playing video games the kids were sitting on their seats for long periods of time which is not really good for them. The games were essentially violent games and violence is not good for the yet-to-mature brains of the kids.

Farishta went around a little more and found the same scene in most of the homes. The kids were busy either with the TV, computer, or video games. Even where the kids went to a babysitter's place, the scene was the same. The TV was on and the little ones were eagerly watching what was showing on the screen. Some were playing video games or computer games. Very rarely were they out in the garden playing together or doing any creative work like making drawings or painting pictures, reading books or doing puzzles. In short, very rarely were they involved in activities where they were active participants, either physically or mentally.

Farishta decided to call it a day and flew back. He wanted to discuss the matter with Almighty at length. A whole new generation was involved and he wanted to know what was going wrong and how. He did not know much himself and needed to ask a lot.

Almighty was leaving for his evening walk when Farishta arrived. He saw the confused look on Farishta's face and smiled, "So today you are unable to make out the relevance of what you just saw. New technology has taken over the lives of little children to a large extent. Instead of playing around and exercising their brains with creative work they are glued to their TV sets or their computers. Children are no longer growing up in the innocent environment they used to. And that is not only making them confused, it is also robbing them of their childhood and is having its negative effect on their growth and development."

"Yes, I too felt so. In most of the homes I visited, the kids were either watching TV or playing video games. Only in rare cases were they engaged in creative or productive work," said Farishta.

Farishta explained to Almighty all that he had seen. He did not know what to make out of it all and wanted Almighty to explain things to him. Though kids everywhere seemed quite happy doing what they did – sitting in front of the TV, playing on the computer, or playing video games, playing outside, making drawings, reading books of their interest. Every activity they were engaged in was enjoyable for them. And the kids who were helping their mother with her work looked even happier. They appeared enthusiastic about what they did and were actively involved with a sense of responsibility and worth. This appeared good for their self-esteem and self-confidence as well. Whatever the kids did, they seemed to like it and Farishta did not know what to make out of it all.

"What is the harm in keeping little children busy one way or the other, they seem to enjoy everything they do? Why is it not right for little kids to watch TV when they like it so much, and, at the same time, it also gives free time to the adults to do their own work? After all, technology is meant to help people," he questioned.

"Technology is no doubt meant to help people, but everything has its own value and drawbacks. Especially where little kids are involved. Childhood is the time when their body, brain, and emotions are developing and every experience leaves a lasting effect on them. Little children generally like everything to start with and then learn to make choices depending on what they are exposed to the most," said Almighty. "The problem with allowing a small child to watch TV is that it engages the child's attention without exercising her brain. This prevents the formation of new neuronal connections in the brain of the child that are essential for critical thinking and language development. People who have studied the effects of TV watching on little kids know that *children under two years of age should not be allowed any TV viewing at all* and they are trying their best to make young parents aware of it. And it is better that the kids do not watch any TV till three years of age. Even after that TV should be restricted to just one hour a day for children up to the age of five. More of it is not good for them even after that," explained Almighty.

"Oh, really?" Farishta was shocked, "I found a lot of parents using TV to keep their kids engaged. It must be affecting their development then," Farishta felt alarmed.

"Yes, excessive TV does a lot of harm to the kids. Child development experts know that the brain grows faster during the first three years of a child's life. This is the time when the child learns to walk, talk, think, and interact with people. Emotional development of the child also takes place at this time. Children who watch too much TV in the early years of life have decreased attention spans and are scholastically backward. They become violent and confused because the programs they watch have a lot of violence and distorted life images that are not good for the maturing brains of the kids. They thus develop a distorted outlook of the world which is likely to stay with them for life.

"TV viewing encourages intellectual passivity in the child for the brain does not get the stimulation it needs. While watching TV, the child is entertained but is not actively involved in the story; the child's brain remains passive for long periods and learns to be so during other activities as well. As a result, when the child grows older, it is less likely to make an effort to play with other kids, take up a hobby, come up with new ideas and plans and be creative. During the early years, sensory, emotional and physical deprivation will retard a child; while over stimulation can make a child restless, discontented and nervous. TV does not take any of these things into account and that can be very harmful to the children affecting their development for life," said Almighty.

"Then it must be disastrous for a small child to watch TV. But why do parents allow them to watch so much TV these days?" asked Farishta, feeling anxious for the little ones and their future.

"You are right," said Almighty, "Parents need to be more aware and careful. And this is what is bothering me a lot. Parents allow their kids to watch TV for a number of reasons that may or may not be easy to address. A lot of times they are not aware of the disastrous effects of it themselves and are happy switching it on to keep the kids engaged and entertained. Then there are some who do know that it is harmful for the kids but are ignorant about the extent of damage it can cause and are thus not keen to restrict its use. And then there are some who are aware but are too busy themselves to be able to do anything about it."

"TV, in any case, cuts down on learning time and playtime of the little ones and that can never be good for them. Children do need a lot of physical and mental activity for proper all round growth. This much even I know," said Farishta.

"Yes, TV viewing comes in the way of physical activity, social interaction, and creative play of the children which deprives them of the opportunity of all round proper growth and development. And lack of physical activity is also contributing to obesity in children which is becoming a global problem these days," said Almighty, and explained further,

"Besides, when a child watches TV it is the actual change of impulses in the brain that hold the child's attention, not the content or the story. As a result of this, the brain goes blank and stays inactive for as long as the child is watching the small screen uninterrupted. When children get accustomed to fast moving images to hold their attention, they find it difficult to focus their attention on tasks that need sustained attention and mature handling.

"And then, children are also not able to filter out incoming information like adults can. They believe and learn whatever they are exposed to. By watching violence on TV, little children grow up to believe that the world is a bad place and they tend to become either violent or scared. When the kids see violence or rude behaviour working on TV, they catch on the idea and do the same. They can even become so used to violence and rude behaviour that the absence of it may make their world bland and they may want to fantasize it and create it in their minds and then enact it in real life.

"Real world and the world shown on TV are not the same and this confuses the kids and they can grow up to have a much distorted view of life, which, very often, stays with them all through their lives with disastrous consequences. Even kids as old as eight are unable to critically comprehend televised advertising messages and are prone to accept advertiser messages as truthful, accurate and unbiased. The effects of TV viewing on young children can be far reaching and irreversible and parents need to be very careful," said Almighty. He continued after some thought,

"Parents need to understand that for a small child, play is work. The brain develops through play and every experience makes a significant contribution. It is not that only violent programs are harmful on TV. As I have told you earlier, TV is also harmful as it turns the mind off. TV shows you the picture as well as tells you the story. Unlike reading a book where you have to imagine what is going on, which keeps the brain active. When the brain remains inactive while its attention is held by the rapidly moving images, it goes in a trance-like state and goes blank. This is very harmful for the rapidly-growing brains of the little ones. Asking questions while watching the tube can break the mesmerizing spell to some extent as it forces the child to think and that activates the child's brain. Parents should be there with the kids and talk to them about the program on the small screen to keep their brains active." Almighty tried his best to explain things to Farishta in detail.

"Then what should the parents do to keep their kids away from the harmful effects of TV? After all, majority of the kids today spend a lot of their time watching the tube, more than any other single activity they do. And the adults are either helpless or do not know the implications, and in a rare case, may not really care," said Farishta realizing the full repercussions of unrestricted TV viewing and feeling concerned for the little ones.

"It is not difficult to keep the kids away from TV if the adults want to," said Almighty. "The only thing is that they have to first understand the harmful effects of letting their kids entertain themselves with TV and then being strict in imposing the needed restriction. There are many ways in which little kids can be kept away from the small screen if the parents are aware of the implications and are prepared to make the needed effort.

"Parents should-

1. Avoid letting kids below three watch any TV at all.
2. Monitor the number of hours their kids watch TV.
3. Decide what programs they can watch and make them stick to the time schedule.
4. Encourage them to see informative programs suited for their age.
5. Be there when the kids are watching TV and talk to them about what they see. This will ensure that the kids get the right message as well as that their brains do not go into a trance.
6. Children should never have a TV installed in their bedrooms.
7. Discourage children from watching TV during meals.

8. Be careful not to watch TV serials or movies when the kids are around. Even when they may not be actively watching them, they still get affected.
9. Parents need to be good role models themselves. They need to restrict their own TV viewing.
10. Parents can have a weekly ban on TV. This will help the little ones to learn how to use their free time better and have control over their whims in favour of their betterment. This will go a long way in adult life.
11. Parents should offer alternative non-screen entertainment like reading books, doing art projects, playing in the garden, doing puzzles, listening or dancing to music, tidying up their room, etc. Helping the parents is also fun for little kids when they do it along with the parents and know that they are making a positive contribution. This will have special value later in adult life; it will help them to be responsible and productive adults who enjoy making positive contributions.

"And it is not just the TV that we are talking about here. Computer games and video games also need to be set in limits. And parents should also monitor what games their kids play."

Almighty explained everything to Farishta in great detail and Farishta was satisfied with the exhaustive information he got today. But it made him more anxious for the little ones and their future.

It was now getting late and Farishta felt tired. More out of worry than anything else. He wanted to freshen up before sitting down for his meal. He decided not to go down the next day and have another round of discussion with Almighty instead. And Almighty invited him for breakfast the following morning. Farishta thanked Almighty, took his leave, and left.

ALMIGHTY TALKS TO FARISHTA

Farishta woke up to a new dawn. He had no plans to go down to the earth today; he wanted to have an exclusive one to one talk with Almighty instead. He had a lot to ask and it would take time.

As usual, Almighty had readily agreed to answer all his queries. Farishta was very excited. He rushed through his morning chores with lightning speed and joined Almighty for breakfast. The spread in front of him was heavenly but his mind was not there. He was not interested in eating, he just wanted to listen to what Almighty had to say. And almighty obliged him to his satisfaction.

Almighty was in a reflective and somber mood. The world he had created with such care and confidence to be a replica of heaven was being messed up by the very people he had placed his faith in. He had given humans the most beautiful and bountiful planet in the whole universe to live in and enjoy. He had also given them a wonderful thinking brain that could reflect and reason for itself and even improve upon it in every way. This has given humans the power to rule the planet and make life easy and comfortable. But has this contributed to more happiness and satisfaction in life? Happiness and satisfaction are the ultimate aim of all human endeavour and that is what appears to be getting lost. What a pity!

Every new generation of humans is supposed to be an improvement over the pervious one and take the world ahead, both scientifically and spiritually. But somehow something appears to be going wrong. At the emotional and spiritual levels, humans are unable to keep pace with their scientific growth and development. In the rat race of their phenomenal scientific development and material success, they are getting trapped in a selfish mind-set where they cannot see beyond their own interest and are trying to get ahead in whatever way possible. They are somehow falling short in their life skills and value systems that are in direct proportion to happiness and peace of mind. Human values have taken a back seat, and when human values go down, nothing else has much meaning either. This is taking its toll and spoiling their new generation.

It is not that humans do not have the power to think and reason for themselves, or they do not want to relax and enjoy what they have and what they have achieved. After all, every effort they make is ultimately aimed at making them happy at some level or the other. There is phenomenal scientific growth and development in the world today and people are also putting in a lot of hard work. But at the emotional and spiritual levels, humans seem to have taken a knock.

But aren't humans a wise species capable of judging their own actions and the results they bring? Then why are they not trying to match their human qualities with their scientific growth? Why are they unable to help their kids to grow up into mature and responsible adults, who can, not only lead happy and meaningful lives themselves, but can make everyone else happy too? And we know that happiness is the ultimate aim of all mankind and every human enterprise.

Almighty has given humans lovely little kids whom they can help to grow up to be responsible and mature adults capable of living rewarding and blissful lives. This can bring the greatest contentment and fulfillment to the parents. After all, what can be more satisfying than to see your child grow up to be a successful and responsible adult. But somehow something is going horribly wrong.

"The main problem with humans" said Almighty "is that they do not always think of the result their actions would bring, though they very well know that every action has a consequence. I have not only given humans an extraordinary brain, I have also given them this unique power to be able to analyze their own actions like a third person and work on them for their own betterment. They can learn either from their own experiences or from the experiences of others and modify their behaviour according to their needs. Or they can even imagine, speculate and come up with new ideas and solutions. But instead of making use of this very special ability, humans seem to think that they are so extraordinary and smart that they do not have to adhere to the natural laws of life. They want to have all their whims and fancies fulfilled in whatever way possible and think they will be able to get away with whatever they do. This is what they are inadvertently teaching their children which is turning out to be a major problem today."

"You are right," said Farishta, "I have seen that parents try to fulfil every demand of their children and allow them to make their own choices which may not always be sensible. They want to make their children happy at any cost; they do not think of the long term consequences of irresponsible behaviour learnt in childhood. Do you think the parents are not doing their duty well?" he asked.

"The problem is not with the intentions of the parents; it is with the way they are going about their duties and responsibilities that needs to be looked into," said Almighty and continued, "As you have just said, the modern-day parents believe that every demand of their kids should be met and children should be allowed to make their own choices from the very beginning. They very wrongly believe that this would raise the confidence level of their kids and prepare them to face the challenges of the world better. They do not realize that children have to be first taught what good choices are and how to make them before they should be allowed to have their way.

"In the absence of parental guidance and the burden of making choices without proper understanding, children learn to make random choices without thought or rationale, and then continue to do so in adult life. It becomes a way of life with them which can, very often, lead to unfortunate consequences. Besides trying to make their children happy, it is also easier for the parents to let the children have their way. Disciplining a child can, at times, need a lot of understanding and effort which the parent may not always be keen to make.

"When children are allowed to make random choices without proper guidance, they do not develop the capability of understanding the pros and cons of their actions and preferences. They do not learn to differentiate between right and wrong and believe that just anything will work, their desires are supreme. When they get into trouble as kids, their parents rescue them and they do not learn to be accountable for their actions either. Irresponsible behaviour then gets endorsed as a way of life and they find it difficult to grow up to be responsible adults. This very understandably comes in their way of success and happiness later on in life. And, as you know, success is a prerequisite to happiness and happiness is the ultimate aim of all mankind. You have to first make some meaningful contribution before you can feel satisfied and contended. You can never be both successful and happy by being indiscrete, demanding, and self-centered. The worst thing parents can do to their children is to pamper them and teach them no discipline," said Almighty, sounding reflective and unhappy.

'This is a very serious matter," agreed Farishta. "I can fully appreciate your concern. Parents do appear confused these days. With better exposure and more knowledge, people can easily help their kids to develop stronger and better values that are necessary for living happier and successful lives. But I cannot understand one more thing," Farishta continued, "The outside world is the same for every child, then how does it affect her in different ways? What role do parents have in it and how does it work?" he asked.

"The first thing the parents have to keep in mind is that the kids are smarter than they think they are. Their brains are very receptive and perceptive, and extremely impressionable too. If this was not so, they would not be able to learn so much so fast that they need to," said Almighty and continued,

"Whatever they experience and see in the initial years of life gives them their first idea of what it could be and a certain meaning gets attached to it in the process. Their mind then perceives similar situations through its first impression and interprets them accordingly. Every first experience in the life of a child is important, even before the age of one year. Children do not remember their first experience even though it leaves its mark on them and this is what makes it difficult for them to know where the fault lies and how to set it right. And they continue to repeat their behaviour even if it does not bring the desired result. No doubt the world out there is the same for every child, but it affects them in different ways because different people attach different meaning to the same incident and see the world differently. What you interpret and perceive is what your reality is, irrespective of the fact that it may be completely different.

"You know that different kids choose different company and get influenced in diverse ways. The reason for this is obvious once you understand how. When a child comes into the world, its mind is largely fresh except for a few prenatal experiences that do have a little meaning but are not significant enough in most cases. In a fresh mind, every experience assumes a greater meaning for it gives the child an idea of what a situation like this is. The child then learns to give similar meaning to similar situations. When these situations are repeated over time, a certain meaning gets attached to them and the child then learns to interpret and respond to similar looking situations in the same manner even though they may not really be the same and may not even bring the same result.

"For example, a child who grows up amongst responsible and good people grows up to have faith in the basic goodness of all despite a few unhappy experiences later on in life. While the one who grows up in the company of irresponsible and selfish people grows up to interpret everyone to be so even though she may, later on, come across exceptionally good people. This is where the importance of early years lies. And that is how 'individual nature' of the children is formed and the parents wonder how they got influenced and what role they had," explained Almighty trying his best to make Farishta understand this complex situation which is, in spite of being so simple, a little difficult to understand.

"Now I understand how and why everything a child witnesses at home is so important. Then it should also be easy to help a child to grow into a responsible and caring adult if the parents take care to set the right examples. Now tell me what do you want the parents to do so that their children grow up to become responsible adults they can be proud of? After all, that is the dream of every parent," Farishta was curious.

"A very important thing parents should do, apart from setting the right examples, is to assign responsibility to their kids from a very early age," said Almighty. "It is a crucial skill children develop at home and early in life. I emphasize the need for responsibility because it is an essential quality needed for accomplishments in life later. And the sooner you start, the better it is. No irresponsible and unaccountable person with no idea of the consequences of one's action can do anything significant.

"Even two-year-olds can be asked to help in clearing their toys and you will find that they will be happy to do it and have fun too. Chores help kids to become active members of their families and bond better with it. When a toddler helps to sweep with a baby broom, or brings a nappy for an infant sibling, he gets a feeling of pride in his work as it enhances his self-worth in his eyes which goes a long way in making him a contributing member of the family and the society.

"Parents should also help their kids to develop an intrinsic feeling of satisfaction. Children should never be tempted with rewards or goodies or be over-praised, or else they will learn to behave responsibly only when they can be rewarded for it in some way or the other. And that does not work later in life when your basic worth becomes more important. Responsibility helps the kids to feel they are a useful part of the unit, be it family or school. Their self-esteem goes up and they feel satisfied and happy. And that is real reward in itself, which stays with them as their own and is neither dependent on outside forces, nor can it be taken away. Even when they get no outside acknowledgment of their contribution, they still know it and their inner self keeps them satisfied.

"Child guidance experts have been telling parents this for a long time and I hope they listen to them. Access to knowledge is very easy now," Almighty said with hope.

"Yes, access to knowledge is very easy these days, but a lot of parents may still not have enough of it. Can you please list out some important points you want the parents to know that will help them to raise responsible kids? That will make things easier for me to understand as well," enthused Farishta and Almighty obliged-

"Yes I can, if you want" he said and went on-

1. The first and foremost thing that parents should do is to model responsible behaviour for their kids for that is what they will learn from them.
2. Start young. Even before the child is two years old. This is the time when the child is most receptive to learning. Eighteen months olds can also pick up their toys and give them to the adult to tidy up the room and you will find that they will take delight in it as well.
3. Establish boundaries. Rules and boundaries provide direction and give confidence to the child to explore the world better.

4. Believe in your kids. Whatever the parents expect from their children, they live up to it. That is important for their development and self-worth. But never shower them with undeserved praise; it will rob them of inner self-esteem which is an essential quality needed for success and happiness in life.
5. Teach self-control and discipline. Self control has to be learnt early in life and is an essential quality. Learning to be able to delay gratification goes a long way. If you satisfy all your child's whims and fancies at once, then she will never learn to delay gratification and that can become a major problem later on in life.
6. Do not tempt the little ones with rewards and goodies all the time or else they will not develop a natural sense of responsibility and self worth.
7. Instill respect for others. That is an essential quality of people who are great achievers. There is so much a person needs to learn form the world and other people and work with them too. And if you do not respect others, you will not be able to learn new ideas and thoughts and grow and function properly.
8. Play with your kids and talk to them. Try to know their friends and their parents. It will not only make them more confident that you care for them and are involved; it will also help you to look after them better and know them better.
9. Inculcate a proper value system in your kids. A human life deficient in values can be very frustrating and difficult. The beauty of human life lies in its

values, and if they are ignored, nothing worthwhile remains.

10. And above all, never forget that you are a parent and not just a friend. You are the only parent (mother or father) your child has and she needs you as such. Never take the easier way out and try to be just a friend. Being a parent is far more difficult but far more challenging, important, and satisfying too. And it is your duty to do your duty well. Parents who feel responsible for their kids' behaviour are more effective parents and their children tend to behave more responsibly,"

Said Almighty summing it up for the benefit of young parents and Farishta too.

"Now I fully appreciate your concern and I also realize that it is not at all difficult to raise responsible kids one can be proud of. It is just that the parents have to be aware and take their responsibility more seriously and go about it the right way. No doubt, responsible parents have responsible kids. I hope all young parents understand their role in raising their kids and do a better job of it now. Whatever I have seen and learnt in these few days has been very enlightening and informative and I am thankful to you for that. And above all, now I know that it is not at all difficult to raise responsible kids and they can all be raised to grow up to be responsible and successful adults who can lead satisfying and meaningful lives," enthused Farishta in anticipation.

"I hope your wish comes true and parents learn to take their responsibility more seriously. After all, access to

information is so very easy these days and the parents can get it all in minutes," said Almighty with hope.

"You are right. It is not at all difficult for parents to gather all the information they require. With me the things were different. I was not familiar with the ways of the world and had to go down to understand that first before I knew what was going wrong and how. Besides, it took time for me to assimilate so much of new information so fast," said Farishta.

"That is right. I think the past week has been very exhaustive for you and you need a well-deserved break. Enjoy a good holiday if you like," Almighty advised and got up.

"Yes, I think I should take a break now," said Farishta. "I need some time to assimilate and understand what I have seen and learnt these few days and a break will do me good. I will go on a holiday for a while and meet you after I come back," he said as he stood up, thanked Almighty, and left.

The future destiny of the child is always the work of the mother.
– Bonaparte.